What is Prayer?

Carolyn Nystrom

illustrated by Eira Reeves

Note to adults

References to Bible passages are given on some pages to support the text. You may like to read these verses yourself for additional background when answering a child's questions.

UK edition published 1996 by Scripture Union,
207–209 Queensway, Bletchley, Milton Keynes, Bucks MK2 2EB

Copyright © The Moody Bible Institute of Chicago

Designed by Three's Company, London

ISBN: 1 85999 082 7

Worldwide co-edition organised and produced by Angus Hudson Ltd, Concorde House, Grenville Place, London NW7 3SA

Printed in Singapore

Have you ever talked to God? I have.
Prayer is so special that I want everyone to
know about it.

1

Romans 15:4

You see, God loves me so much that he wants to talk to me. That's why he gave me the Bible.

John 4:23

But God wants me to talk to him too. So in the Bible he tells me how to pray. Prayer is talking to God.

THE BIBLE

THE BIBLE

Friends like to talk to each other. And God
is my friend.

4

Psalm 139:1–12

I can talk to God ANYWHERE about ANYTHING. God always hears and understands.

God hears me if I whisper, or if I shout, or even if I only think a prayer in my mind.

I can pray when I run, when I sit, or when I stand. God still hears.

7

But sometimes I want God to see how I feel about my prayer. I might stand to show God that I respect him.

Dear God
I love to
talk to you
From David

Psalm 95:6; 134:1–2; 1 Timothy 2:8; 2 Samuel 6:14

I might kneel down to show God that I am sorry for doing wrong. I might let my whole body show God how happy I am to know him. God sees and hears and knows what I mean.

Psalm 139:6

I read in the Bible about how great God is.
He knows everything. He sees everywhere. He
can do anything. And God loves me. I praise
him. I say, `God, you are wonderful.'

2 Corinthians 1:11

I thank God for good times with Dad.
  I pray, `Please keep Dad strong and healthy.'

James 5:14–15

When my friend Bobby is sick, I ask God to
be close to him.
   I pray, `God, please help Bobby.'
And he does.

Philippians 4:6

When I think about going to school, I worry about what sort of teacher I'll have.

I pray, `God, I'm scared. Please give me a kind teacher.'

And Miss Newman is just great.

But I don't always please God. I get angry at Bobby. Or I tell my mother I've eaten all my peas when I haven't. Or I won't play with Suzy. Or I play too roughly with my puppy. God isn't happy when I do something wrong.

14

1 John 1:9

So I say, `God, I'm sorry. I'll try not to do it again.' And God forgives me. `

Romans 12:1

I want to show God how much I love him. I pray, `God, I give you a present. It is myself.'

There are many kinds of prayer. Sometimes I pray a short prayer about just one thing. Other times I pray all kinds of prayers and talk to God a long time.

1 Thessalonians 5:17

God wants me to talk to him often. In the Bible, he says, 'Pray without ceasing.' That means, 'Pray at all times.'

Matthew 18:19–20

God wants me to pray sometimes with other people. The Bible tells me prayer has great power when two or three pray together.

17

Matthew 6:5–7

God knew I'd want to please him with my prayers. So in the Bible he gave rules for praying. He said: Don't say lots of words that don't mean anything. Don't say the same thing over and over for no reason. Don't pray just to show off.

Matthew 6:9–13

When Jesus was here, he prayed often. Once Jesus' followers asked him to teach them to pray too. He told them, 'Pray like this.'

'Our Father in heaven,
  hallowed be your name,
your kingdom come, your will be done on earth as it is in heaven.
Give us today our daily bread.
Forgive us our debts,
  as we also have forgiven our debtors.
And lead us not into temptation,
  but deliver us from the evil one.
For yours is the kingdom,
and the power, and the glory, for ever. Amen.'

19

Romans 8:26; Jude 20

Even if I'm not sure how to pray, God wants me to pray anyway. The Holy Spirit will make my prayer right.

But sometimes I ask God for something that he does not give. Once I asked God to keep my best friend, Linda from moving away. But Linda moved anyway.

21

So I wondered, *Did God hear?*
Did God care how much I
wanted Linda to stay? Did I ask
something too hard for God?

Psalm 34:17; 1 Peter 5:7; Jeremiah 32:17

Then I remembered, *God hears. God cares. And there is nothing too hard for God.* And I remembered other times when he answered my prayers. I thanked him for those times.

Matthew 17:20

God gives me some reasons in the Bible—
reasons why he does not always give what I
ask.

Perhaps I don't really believe that God will
answer my prayer. I need to trust him more.

Matthew 5:23–24; 6:15

Maybe I am angry at someone who has done wrong to me. I need to make friends again with him.
  Or I might be doing something that displeases God. I need to turn away from that and tell God I'm sorry.

James 4:3

Or maybe God wants me to wait a while
for what I have asked for.

But most likely, God knows that what I ask is
not good for me — or for someone else. And
God knows best. I don't want God to give me
what I ask if he knows it isn't good.

26

Maybe God knows it was better for Linda to move away. God knows I feel sad. I can tell him how I feel.

James 4:2

God listens to every prayer. And God wants to give me good things. But he wants me to ask him. It shows I need and trust him.

God is so big and so good and so
wonderful. And he is my friend. He wants me
to talk to him. That's why I pray.

You can pray too.
God wants to be your friend.